MENTAL ILLNESS DOES NOT EXIST

antipsychiatry: basic operating instructions

BUCALO GIUSEPPE

ISBN: 1499229631
ISBN-13: 978-1499229639
Translated by Emilio Florio and Laura Mazzatenta

MENTAL ILLNESS DOES NOT EXIST

"Who can go out except through the door?
Why, then, does no one follow this way?"
(Confucius)

A man is standing naked in the village square. He shouts his beliefs. One must be freed from matter and become as pure spirit. What happens? Centuries ago we might have had an answer. We would have wondered if the man was 'inhabited' by god or the devil before acting. In a different square from a different country, perhaps we would be sitting in circle trying to hear the words, to decipher the response, to learn from him. Here and now we do not think anything but 'he's unwell' and 'he needs treatment'.

But what does this man 'suffer' from? Perhaps from the frost on this autumn day (which he can't avoid feeling)? Yet he yells out of joy that the time has come, free and ready to fly. Someone suggests that he is 'beside himself' and that 'he does not know what he's doing.' It's not him. It cannot be him.

And we? Do we know what we're doing when we phone the doctors and alert the police? Do we know what those men are actually doing when they cover him and force him to get on an ambulance? Everything we see is a hospital admission: a person that is conducted in a place where he will be helped find his 'sanity'.

A hospital admission. How short our memory is. Didn't we see the same thing while they were taking away Carmelo, Nino, Giuseppina, Sebastiano, Cateno, Giorgio, Sonia, Giovanni...? A hospital admission, a 'treatment' for the cure of the disease of being who one is. And where are they now? Who's back? And what 'cure' have they undergone?

We know what we are doing. The nurses know it while they restrain him down in bed with the bands. The doctors who prescribe the 'treatment' of the case know it. They know they find themselves faced with a mentally ill person suffering from 'mystical delusion' that needs to be brought back to 'reason'. They would not have hesitated to do so with Buddha, Christ, John the Baptist, Teresa of Avila, as well as they did with Van Gogh or Nietzsche, if only they could have had them under observation.

But what does this man suffer from? Does he suffer from the bands around his wrists? Does he suffer at finding himself locked up? At being ridiculed and humiliated by all? At being unheard? No, say his warders, he suffers from the 'disease' of being unaware of being suffering. He is 'ill' because he says he is not. It is clear for us (who know what we are saying) that one cannot be happy at being naked in the middle of a square, one cannot want this; it is neither logical nor acceptable.

The naked man is not Francis of Assisi. It is not a saint, a mystic; he is just a 'mentally ill' whose brain chemistry is 'impaired' for unknown reasons. We are still able to be moved by the Canticle of the Creatures, to be touched by poverty and the Franciscan utopia, but we do not have any doubts on the naked man, on his irrationality. We believe we are able to discern between the holy and the sick, between divine visions and hallucinations, between faith and delusion, between meditation and autism.

What we saw in the pre-psychiatry era as a divine manifestation, we are now ready to swear it is only the 'symptom' of an illness of the nervous system. The voice of god - just a hallucination; the mission of Francis - only a delusion; his nakedness - 'mental illness'.

But what is mental illness? A hypothesis. The idea that it was not the 'voice of god' that stripped down the naked man, but only a pathological process that has altered the 'normal' functioning of his brain. Just a guess. There is not, as of today, any clear evidence of the existence, nature and causes of this process. Yet psychiatrists continue to treat mental illness as a 'fact' and to impose any sort of 'therapies' involuntarily on people.

Psychiatry has never 'cured' anyone. The electroshock, lobotomy, insulin shock, pyro-therapy, psychotropic medication, psychotherapy ... are not cures, but 'experiments' on uninformed living human subjects, and often without consent. With these 'experiments' psychiatry tries to understand what it does and what is pointless to do. The 'logic' is the same of the child who destroys the toy to see how it's done and how it works.

It is not just a metaphor. Psychiatry considers its guinea pigs in the same way of things or, at best, 'laboratory animals'. In his experiments it calmly sacrifices their existences considering them non-lives devastated by the disease. Having 'lost their mind', they are left with nothing to lose. They may be sacrificed. We may try to surgically dissect their brains to find the core of madness. They call it lobotomy; it comes to test if, by removing parts of human beings' brain, they begin to resemble the psycho-surgeon who has operated them, to the point of thanking them for this action. Thousands of people have been destroyed in this way. Reduced to living as vegetables to allow psychiatrists to 'test' their theories and demonstrate the existence of the 'illness' that they claimed to cure. Thousands of non-consenting human beings, who shouted, struggled, scratched, bit, punched and kicked until the last minute, desperate and helpless.

What is this for? For nothing. After decades, psychosurgery was replaced by psychiatric drugs. Surgery was abandoned. The lobotomized were herded in asylums. Afterwards, their doctors were promoted to work in the community, as men of science and medicine.

And we? Where were we? Where we are now: on the roadside to see the naked man of the square being ensnared.

MENTAL ILLNESS DOES NOT EXIST. Every time we venture beyond the permissible limit we raise a firestorm of fear and perplexity. We're not naked, let alone talking to the stones, we cannot bear the burden of disabling diagnoses, however we agree with the naked man, with his 'unreasonable' claim of not being 'sick'.

They say: 'you deny the evidence!' I believe that we simply deny that what is before us is the result of an illness. I see the naked man, I hear him talking to the stones and shouting things I do not understand. I, as well as the psychiatrist, cannot hear what the stones respond; like the psychiatrist, I also have never heard them utter a word. Yet I cannot see an illness. I do not feel his pain. I do not see him trembling in the cold. I do not feel shame in him. I only see his joy. The ecstasy of his gaze.

There are no unbridgeable differences between me and the naked man. We act both according to our experiences, consistently with our own ideas, to reach a purpose. I cannot define him ill only because he lives an experience that I don't know, he believes in things that I do not agree with, or he attempts to obtain results which I consider impossible. I could call him immoral, sinful, dreamer ... that is expressing an ethical and human judgment about him. I might even call him criminal if his conduct violates the criminal laws. But I cannot 'reasonably' call him ill and deny him the desire to be who he is. I could make all these judgments, and be wrong.

The reality of what we see, hear, think is not in our biochemistry. The truth of our experiences is not a product of our brain. We perceive reality through our senses; through our brain we process information. But what we feel, the ideas we conceive, the intentions we have, cannot in any way be reduced to the way our organs work.

I have no difficulty in stating that all human experiences have a biochemical and organic basis. We can see through our eyes, think with our brain, move on our legs ... I am convinced that in the brain of the man who hears the 'voice' of god something happens, something that allows him to hear it, see it, touch it. I am afraid this is not the problem. The question we need to ask is whether and to what extent we can decide that the brain that sees the Coliseum is 'normal' and the one that sees the archangel Gabriel is 'sick'.

The decision on the normality and reality of an idea or experience is not something that concerns medicine. The organic processes are impersonal: they are not right or wrong, true or false, moral or immoral. The decision on what to label as mental illness or mental health has nothing to do with science: it concerns the conscience, the morals, the beliefs of those who arrogate to themselves the power to judge. By defining 'pathological' the ideas that we do not understand, we define 'pathological' the human beings who think and share those ideas.

The case of homosexuality is emblematic of the un-reasoning way of psychiatry. Diagnosed as a mental illness for decades, with the change of morals it is reintegrated into the world of sanity. This disease disappears from the psychiatric diagnostics with the same rapidity with which every year new diseases become part of it. Virtually all behaviours that have lost citizenship in the social community go on psychiatric records; those who are gradually digested leave psychiatric records.

What does all this have to do with scientific research, with biochemistry, with genetic studies? Can we 'reasonably' believe that there are 'sick' ideas and 'healthy' ideas? The former delivered by an 'altered' mind, the latter by a 'normal' mind? And what distinguishes them? The fact of being or not being shared? Of producing pain or joy? Of being unprovable? Of denying the laws of physics?

According to the parameters we 'normally' use to define a 'sick' idea, we might say that the faith in the existence of the soul or a god creator of heaven and earth is the result of 'sick minds'. It is indeed unprovable, it transcends and denies physical laws, it has produced untold suffering (fear, guilt, Holy Inquisition ...) and, for a long time, it was the idea of persecuted minorities. All the religions of the world are only 'sick' ideas that have tainted the minds of millions of human beings. Believers of all faiths are motivated by personal and collective experiences that psychiatrists call 'delusional' and 'hallucinatory'.

What is the difference between the biochemistry of Mary who hears and sees the angel announcing her divine mission, and the biochemistry of the naked man to whom the angel announced the end of the world? And between their chemistry and the one of the psychiatrist who says that angels do not exist and there is mental illness? All three see things that cannot be proven. The difference lies not in their biochemistry, but in the degree of agreement that communities express towards each of these 'faiths'. Mary - and her experience - is neutralized by being relegated into the symbolic, the psychiatrist deals with the real; the naked man is left with just a bed in hospital.

I have no doubt that one day psychiatric research can establish, at least in part, the chemical and biological mechanisms that have allowed Francis of Assisi to be who he is, what has extended his hearing until he understood the language of animals, what has allowed him to reproduce their language, what has refined his sight to the point of seeing the streets that go through the roof into the infinite.

The question is not whether and to what extent his biochemistry is altered. The problem is whether we consider him 'acceptable'. Will we accept his experience or find it intolerable, weird, and dangerous? Will we consider that it is a step on the path to perfection or a useless fantasy? Will we accept that our children go wandering on the roof and talk to the pigeons and cats, risking to fall down, that they stop working, washing and dressing, that they free themselves of all the gifts with which we were able to fill their lives? The paradox in which we live means that people, who now identify with Francis of Assisi, consider these behaviours as diseases and symptoms of mental illness. The naked man on the street and the man on the roof are not on the path of liberation but on the path of nonsense.

The decision with regards to the future of certain people and experiences will not be made by science, but it will be made by our own fear. Fear is the motor and the purpose of psychiatry. Not knowledge. Fear that everything gets out of hand.

Who decided that our way of living is the only one and this is the only possible world? It is us who construct reality. Not only because we see only what we want to see, but also because we see only what we can see. The colours, shapes, sounds, smells do not exist. They are built by our senses. What we call reality is nothing but a partial picture we create of what is outside or inside us. Is there a 'healthy' way to perceive reality? Or are there endless possibilities of perception? Hearing sounds that others do not hear and seeing things that others do not see, can be capacities and opportunities that are 'superior' to the usual perceptions. With the same arrogance with which we affirm the insanity of these experiences, we could affirm their divinity. Why are they 'sick' and not 'saint'? Why 'crazy' and not 'enlightened'?

Albert tore ten million to pieces, Sandro has stopped the traffic while immerse in the light of revelation, Nino has struggled all night with demons. We say we are available to let others live, to let them be free to believe in their fantasies and their visions, but we would like they didn't do this sort of things. We would appreciate they didn't endanger their (or others') social position, disturb our sight or our hearing, show their beliefs, involve us in their rituals. We would like they were accountants of the absolute, Sunday shamans, scholars of religious mysticism. We have lost cognition of what it means to exit reality in order to enter the truth.

After we are called we are not the same. It is no longer a matter of believing in certain ideas, but being in a new dimension. This is not a matter of creating beliefs or rituals, but being, actualising or defending oneself. There is no human person who has exceeded the limit of human perception and has not irretrievably lost oneself.

If god calls, it never asks for reasoning: it asks you to give up yourself, your resources, your loved ones, your home, the reality. If god calls, it entrust you with a mission in the world, a revelation that you have to bring in every corner of creation, you daring and fearless witness of the sacred. You are not afraid of jail, of the madhouse, of wandering hungry in a train station yanked off by the police, as well as the first Christian martyrs were not afraid of ending up as food for the lions. It's the law of things: each genuine vocation brings a blind and genuine persecution. We become a door opened by the wind of truth, that all are scrambling to close. They don't tear us apart anymore because they realized that, by unhinging us from our hinges, they have left open cracks that can no longer be closed. They close the doors, they lock us out, they build walls around our doors, they twist the senses and the heart of human beings, making them unable to hear what we say. Sometimes it just comes to wonder if they could, with proper psychotherapy and psychiatric support, have persuaded Francis to return to work with his father in Assisi or Prince Siddhartha to resume his royal place in this world of suffering. If they would have been able to confuse them so as to make them come back to reality.

Psychiatrists draw an illusory line between sane and insane people. They think they are able to discern whether an idea is deliberately designed and built by a person, irrespective of what they say. The idea that, so to speak, 'thinks itself alone' is sick, it thinks on behalf of the person who is a victim of it. Mental illness is therefore presented as a sort of mutiny where our head starts to reason on its own. It is a suggestive and arbitrary assumption. From time to time, in fact, the psychiatrist will decide whether and to what extent a person knows what they say, know what they do, think what they say. They will be ill when they say they are healthy and healthy when they accept to be ill. They will be healthy when they agree they need treatment, and sick when they assert that the treatment to which they are subject is actually torture and the physicians are torturers.

Those who are scandalized by asylum violence and claim both the existence of mental illness and the need for a cure, are in a dead end. They try to let out of the window what they receive with all the honours through the front door. If there is such a thing as mental illness that devastates the mind and behaviour of the individual, there shall be something like psychiatry that isolates and controls it. Moreover, we will need psychiatry to decide on behalf of the ill person who, as such, is incapable of deciding on their own existence, the places in which to live and have fun, the right people to meet, the right books to read, the right things to buy, the number of cigarettes to smoke and so forth.

Each 'patient' will be assigned to a psychiatrist who will use any means that their science puts at their disposal to force them to accept reality. No matter how the psychiatrist is mediocre, violent or inhumane, they will always have a 'reason'. They may treat the patient in every way they believe appropriate: no one will stop, accuse, and condemn them, just as no one has condemned those responsible for the horrors of mental hospitals. On the contrary, all psychiatrists who were working in mental asylums have advanced their careers and they have enjoyed their retirement after decades of hard work in which they destroyed the lives of thousands of people.

Such a lack of con(science) needs places where to lock up involuntary patients. Rooms where they can be accommodated and be protected from 'themselves' and 'reality '. Houses with doors that can be locked 'for their own sake'. Laboratories where psychiatrists can study the evolution of the disease. Surgeries where they can test their miracle drugs. Whitewashed places, single rooms, shiny floors, paintings on the walls, radiators ... Places where no psychiatrists would live but that they believe the best place for their patients.

They are called mental health services: they are places where good people continue to do what was done in a mental asylum. They write medical records, they decide what works and what needs to change in you, they come to pick you up and they hospitalize you, they try to cure your sensitivity, they deny the truth to what you say, they know nothing of what you feel, they certify your being delusional... they isolate you.

MENTAL ILLNESS DOES NOT EXIST. And the Monster of Florence[1]? For a perverse mechanism we reckon that our denial that the mind can become sick is outright equivalent to absolve all of the monsters, real or alleged, that populate our daily lives. It's a paradox. In fact the opposite is true. To define mentally ill someone who commits crimes, means to affirm they are guiltless, a non-suit ruling, a verdict of not guilty. Where mental illness is, in fact there is no responsibility. The monster who killed his mother does not know what he is doing; he is not a perpetrator but a victim of his illness: how can we judge and condemn him? Fit of madness, here is the real murderer. The monster is a victim: we have to lock up the monster and cure him.

The monster must not be simply caught, punished and locked up, we want him to be 'cured', those thoughts of his that led him to act to be eradicated, all the reasons that were born inside his mind to be destroyed. What is the real danger? What or whom does the matricide threaten? What makes his reasoning a delusion and what makes the massacre at Bologna station[2] logic even

---

[1] The Monster of Florence, also known as Il Mostro, is an epithet commonly used for the perpetrator, or the perpetrators, of 16 murders that took place between 1968 and 1985 in the province of Florence, Italy.

[2] The Bologna massacre (Italian: Strage di Bologna) was a terrorist bombing of the Central Station at Bologna, Italy, on the morning of 2 August 1980, which killed 85 people and wounded more than 200.

though it is a logic of terror? What makes us say that it is logical to kill a stranger in a war or for money and pathological to kill a loved one for love or hatred?

To say that a particular behaviour makes sense does not mean to accept it. To recognize the meaning does not mean to endorse it. On the contrary, it is often the only way we have to understand it, fight it, and change it. To say that 'it makes sense' to kill one's own mother does not mean it's right, fair or good. Neither more nor less than saying that the Nazi persecution of Jews made sense. The fact that our actions make sense or not, is not to say outright whether they are right or not.

I would try to dissolve the paradox. What's the point in saying that certain actions do not make sense? Who needs it? What is this protecting us from?

Take the case of the matricide. It's not the danger of the act that makes us afraid, or not only. Maybe we are more troubled by the thought that this was possible. By the fact that one of the principles that underpin our sense of reality can be torn into pieces in a moment with awareness and reason. We cannot accept to acknowledge the status of reasoning person in someone

---

The attack has been materially attributed to the neo-fascist terrorist organization Nuclei Armati Rivoluzionari. Suspicions of the Italian secret service's involvement emerged shortly after, due to the explosives used for the bomb and the political climate in which the massacre occurred (the strategy of tension), but have never been proven.

who kills his own mother, while we have no difficulty in believing the killer of the Mafia or the creators of the atomic bomb mission to Hiroshima are sound and sensible (to the point of psychiatrizing the pilot of that flight to Hiroshima diagnosing him mentally ill because oppressed by guilt).

In fact our only priority is to create an unbridgeable gap between us and the matricide. A psychological gap, even more than a physical one. Between him and us there must be no connection. The matricide is not only violating a criminal law: he attacks reality. He opens a deep hole in the veil of Maya, which protects our normality. A bit like the maniac who is masturbating on street corners. He is not breaking a written law; he is showing the disturbing nature of our desires and our passions.

It seems a paradox, but there's nothing more meaningful than to kill those who gave us life. Deleting the first cause, the origin, the door through which we have been thrown into this world. Certainly it makes more sense than killing people whom we do not know and that we were ordered to kill.

We can be reassured by the fact of thinking of such acts as 'pathological' aberrations, exceptions, diseases. It takes them away from us. It keeps us safe from any possible involvement. But all the terror we feel when we are faced with these crimes is the terror of recognizing them as our human and tragic possibilities.

The bonds between people are of a nature that it is impossible at times to discern victims and victimizers. Bonds and homes that often protect and sometimes imprison. Ties and feelings that keep us alive but that sometimes we cannot do without. Sometimes we find no way out unless we cut them off or carry them with us after death. We cannot bear to leave them behind and sometimes we cannot even bear that they do without us.

Here too. What has this fragility and anxiety of ours to do with medicine? What can make us reason? What can prevent us from being human and, therefore, dangerous to ourselves and to others?

I do not condone what at times we can do to one another (with or without bloodshed): I just say that there is nothing that can make us immune from passion without killing us; there is nothing that can make us reason without stopping us to be who we are.

So is psychiatry: it creates the monsters and then it claims to keep them under control.

Psychiatrists tell us a story that we need to believe. They say that behind certain tragic and unacceptable actions there is nothing but a disease, the alteration of some biochemical process, a sick mind. They delude us that by identifying the people who are affected, by isolating and treating them early, they will not commit those actions.

With this logic they were allowed to restrain and control for decades hundreds of thousands of men and women who have never harmed anyone, alleged perpetrators of crimes they never committed. To be called mentally ill is tantamount to being marked as dangerous and brutal criminals.

If we used the same logic against psychiatrists we would probably come to the same conclusion: they are biologically and, probably, genetically dangerous to themselves and others.

In this field, reality and the objective evidence we can bring are worthless. It's no use to point out that the percentage of crimes committed by persons diagnosed as mentally ill is similar (if not less) than the percentage of the same crimes committed by persons considered to be healthy (including psychiatrists). We have the same chance of being killed, robbed, injured by persons whom we consider to be sane or insane. Yet we feel the dangerousness as a fundamental characteristic of illness, and not health.

In fact there is nothing meaningful in our relationship with what and with whom we do not understand. Psychiatry itself is a heap of irrationality and violence, systematized and accepted as obvious.

Mental hospital and psychiatric therapies have never prevented the murderous rampages (which by definition are unpredictable). They just used these acts to justify a crime even bigger: a kind of genocide that has involved (and involves) millions of human beings deprived of any freedom of choice.

MENTAL ILLNESS DOES NOT EXIST. We do not deny reality. We affirm that there are experiences and people who wrong-foot us with their reasoning and behaviour. These are people and experiences we want to have a relationship with, coexist with and share the meaning with. We do not believe that people (mis)treated by psychiatrists are sick, as we do not believe a priori that they suffer from their experiences. We believe that the only way out of the abuse is to accept the self-definition that people give of their situation. The naked man does not suffer his nakedness. He surely is suffering what we do to him in the name of a support that is just mindless violence.

There is no human experience enjoyable and positive in itself. All experiences can be doors to enter heaven or to be thrown into hell. The same experiences, at different times of our lives, can exalt or depress us. We can, likewise, be comfortable with ourselves and be persecuted by others for this. Going through hell, because of our happiness and fullness of life.

Hearing the voice of god can throw you in the darkest terror or uplift you to the most sublime ecstasy. Falling in love can make you feel in heaven or wear you out like a wet rag. For love one can build or destroy homes. Our passion can make us heal incurable diseases or can force us to kill and kill ourselves. And so on.

By saying that the naked man is sick, that Cesare suffers lying on the floor, that Antonio is in agony wandering around the station all night long talking with people we do not see, we justify their involuntary imprisonment. We do not respond to their suffering, but to our suffering. The shame, helplessness, fear, misunderstanding, terror are ours. If Francis is sitting on the roof in the bliss of his relationship with creation, we don't think of bringing some food to allow him to stay there as long as he wants, instead we help him to get down with the help of the fire brigade and, moreover, we help him forget those fantasies and resume his place in reality.

Certainly not everybody trouble us with their bliss. Some people rush into our arms for help, begging us to protect them from entities, monsters and demons that we cannot see. And how do we help them? We tell them that there is nobody, that those are just fantasies, that there is something that does not run well in their biochemistry, maybe stress, maybe some trauma ... and we leave them alone to face demons, we preclude them from any way out, we lock them up in protected places where they cannot escape anywhere.

We are so blind as to not understand that our bid to

avoid making sense of what's happening, is indeed the door to get people into more uncontrollable terror. The psychiatric explanation actually explains nothing, helps no one and serves only the purpose of justifying what the staff will do to you. Sometimes the alternative that we give to those who ask for help is between being torn by demons and being invaded by psychiatric drugs. Out of the frying pan into the fire, as usual.

If there is suffering in human experience, this, in my opinion, is always linked to the ability to understand and make others understand what we want or what is happening to us. Psychiatry does not really know anything about what happens to its users, nor does it appear to be interested in helping them to understand: its sole purpose is to eliminate by any (more or less) permissible means any conduct that is detrimental to the (in)civil community.

I believe that this blindness stems from a logic that says: the sufferings caused by fantasies or imagined realities are themselves imaginary. There's no empathy for the running man chased by demons. We block him. We give him two pats on the back and then off to the nearest hospital emergency room.

It's not us who deny the reality of people that are suffering, but those who believe that people are suffering from mental illness do deny that. By getting rid of the illness we get in touch with the heart of the problem. No one suffers from a disease that others say he is suffering from; we suffer in front of what we do not understand or, even worse, by being systematically misunderstood or ridiculed by others.

ANTIPSYCHIATRY
basic operating instructions

"We will not raise the question of arbitrary confinement. This will save you the trouble of making hasty denials. But we categorically state that a great number of your inmates, quite mad by official definition, are also arbitrarily confined.
We protest against any interference with the free development of delirium. It is as legitimate, as logical as any other sequence of human ideas or acts [...]
We simply affirm that their concept of reality is absolutely legitimate, as are all the acts resulting from it."

(Antonin Artaud)

We learnt the hard way that psychiatry is a sort of border, an invisible line beyond which one loses any right and possibility to exist, a gateway from reality to the impossible. A border, a wall, a straightjacket, paralysing medications, words to forget about it.

We learnt it the hard way by being victims, persecutors or instigators. We have been harmed and we have harmed others and ourselves as much as we possibly can, just to prevent that some of us could cross that border and come back with the treasure, the terror, the astonishment or the fear that they found on the other side.

Antipsychiatry is, therefore, the search of possible ways to cross this border and to rub this line out.

No more distinction between sane and insane mind, instead a new mind that is able to function on both sides of this border.

Let's be clear. Antipsychiatry is Giorgio, his hands holding tight the steering wheel of the bus, the engine turned on and that wall in front of him. He knows that he will pass through it as if it was a wall of fog. He will demonstrate that reality is only the veil of Maya, an illusion, an institution. Giorgio who wants to cut a crack, a wound, a doubt open in the wall of reality. Giorgio, with the engine already turned on and his decision already made.

Antipsychiatry throws down the gauntlet to us, reality and reason. It gives up curing, normalizing or punishing those who don't agree with our way of life. It is the acceptance of the risk of losing one's mind and being pilloried for this.

Antipsychiatry is not an alternative to psychiatry, it's something else. It is an antidote to the psychiatric poison. *Anti* because, in the present age, psychiatry has taken possession of the border, it controls it, it charges an inhuman fee, it imprisons us on both sides of the wall.

Antipsychiatry doesn't aim at replacing psychiatry with human *treatments* or welcoming *places*. It rather deals with the acceptance and the defence of the validity of every human experience and reality. It doesn't involve medicine or psychology; it's a movement of minds and hearts, of human beings who want to explore themselves and reality without taking anything for granted. It is the uneasiness of those who don't accept to stop Giorgio before it's too late, of those who don't accept to label him *ill*, therefore destroying his reasons, his future and his life. It is the agony of those who struggle with themselves to jump on Giorgio's bus and, with him, go beyond.

The history of antipsychiatry walks with Carmelo's legs. It breathes with him, his heart in his mouth, the adrenaline flowing. Night-time, 1962. Carmelo wanders quietly through the ward. He walks up to the beds. He tries to untie his fellow inmates. *"I can't stand seeing them in this way"*, he will tell the doctor who asks him the reasons for that insane deed. *"He can't stand seeing them in this way"*, the psychiatrist writes in his records. Then the order comes. Carmelo gets tied to his bed.

I can't stand seeing them in this way. Carmelo wasn't the only one in those years. A fierce multitude of young mental health professionals would reject the idea of being part and accessory of that genocide that was perpetrated in the mental institutions. They didn't stand the idea of being themselves the ones who gave that order or who gave somebody a death sentence with their judgement. They were known as antipsychiatrists. They were men and women who refused to abide to the mandate that was given to them by society and by the psychiatric moral (ir)responsibility.

Franco was one of them. He was fighting to set Carmelo and his fellow inmates free from the straps that would tie them to their beds. Carmelo would observe him. He would watch that brave hero getting inflamed every time that he succeeded in convincing himself and the nurses that it was possible to release somebody. Cruel paradox. The deed that cost Carmelo months of punishments, degradation and tortures was now acclaimed as a just, human, curative action. That, which in Carmelo was stigmatized as a "symptom" of his mental decline and disease, was seen in Franco as a meaningful and therapeutic action. The same nurses who tied him that night, were untying him today using the same logic, the same arrogance, the same power as always.

Franco would continue the tradition of abuse that Carmelo knew well. He would decide who could be untied and when. Who could be discharged, when and where they were allowed to go. Carmelo's life and that of his fellow inmates still depended on Franco's mood, on his capacity to empathize, to understand, to be convinced.

So Carmelo was buried in a mental institution, while

Franco is today the head doctor of a modern psychiatric ward, built under the precepts of the new psychiatry. On the windows no bars, only shatterproof glass. No straightjacket, only drugs mixtures. The same diagnoses. The same white coats. The same straps. The same order. Arturo is tied to his bed. He attempted to abscond by breaking the handles of the windows tonight.

The antipsychiatric practice isn't dead, only these professed antipsychiatrists who have inherited and re-invented the mental asylum infection, have disappeared.

Antipsychiatry is, in fact, that visceral, instinctive, indestructible thread that unites Carmelo and Arturo, their anger, their reasons, their resistance to the attempt to deny them as human beings. The operating instructions of antipsychiatry come from this heritage of stories and lives that were destroyed by the various psychiatric "revolutions" which have occurred leaving the psychiatric error/horror unchanged.

Psychiatry stays always the same as itself. It doesn't matter if it doesn't build asylums anymore, doesn't promote internment or doesn't practice lobotomy. The problem is not *where* one is locked in or *what* one is allowed to do, to have and to feel, but it's the fact that others decide for us what we can say, think or be.

Antipsychiatry is a way of taking back one's life, one's city, one's future. Carmelo doesn't negotiate for his freedom of movement: he unties himself. Arturo doesn't beg for his right to live where and with whom he wants; he breaks down the windows which keep him imprisoned.

Antipsychiatric action is the coming out from psychiatric domination and abuse: unconditionally. It's not possible to give up one's values, one's sensitivity, one's memories or feelings and to obtain in exchange only a semblance of probation.

Antipsychiatry is Nino's retreat in Pietraperciata's caves. It's the sound of his stick that beats on the world's heart. It's his dream journey between Taormina and his *alter ego*. There's nothing that can bring him back to *reason*, without denying the reality and truth of what he says he is, he feels and he does; without wiping out his being a person; without abusing his body and torturing his mind.

For Nino there's no difference whatsoever between being locked up in an insane asylum or being attended to at home, under house arrest or in probation. There's no difference between lobotomy and psychotropic drugs; between a *schizophrenia* verdict expressed by a mental hospital psychiatrist and the one formulated by a *democratic* psychiatrist[3] or a *psychotherapist*. All of them

---

[3] **Democratic Psychiatry** was the movement for liberation of the people from segregation in mental hospitals by pushing for the Italian psychiatric reform. It was created by a group of left-orientated psychiatrists, sociologists and social workers under

consider their mind, their choices, their life the *norm*. All of them take for granted that Nino can't be the one he claims to be, or do what he does. All of them justify their actions stating that they act in order to help him to alleviate his sufferings. All of them cover up, with their theories, the fact that all that effort essentially serves the purpose of alleviating the sufferings that Nino, with his behaviour, causes to his family, his neighbourhood, and his mental health workers.

Antipsychiatry is the act of coming face to face with Nino beyond the limits of what is *possible*. Walking next to him without imposing a destination. Looking for intersections between our lives and our worlds. Helping him to practice his *madness* and to communicate the knowledge of it.

Sometimes, looking back at the stories of involuntary psychiatric patients, one has the clear impression that, in order to save thousands of people's lives, it would have been enough to *refrain from doing*. It would have been enough if we didn't take responsibility for them so that they at least had a chance to live and die with some sense, as it is the right of every human being.

FIRST INSTRUCTION: DO NOT INTERFERE

I would be tempted to propose *"do not interfere"* as the first instruction. The invasion that we have carried out in

direction of Franco Basaglia. (Translators' Note)

the lives and to the detriment of people we don't comprehend (and experiences we don't know) was so systematic and inhumane that the first sensible thing to do would be to refrain from *doing good actions* for others. One step back. To respect, to keep one's eyes open, to listen to others' experiences without interfering.

I know very well that, in the field of human relations *not interfering* is impossible. The reciprocal action and influence is inherent to our being human. This *in-difference* between us is neither possible, nor desirable. Knowing that a beloved person is wandering at night in the city on a quest to find the Holy Grail can't make us feel comfortable. At least because we don't know what it means, to what it can lead, and, above all, we can't imagine what could happen. It's humanly impossible for us *not to act*. Sure. But there is a way of acting *against*, denying, racing to try and make one change direction, closing doors and windows, putting others' reasons to sleep, imprisoning... *interfering*, wherein someone else's voice, thoughts, aim, don't make sense anymore. Where there is no *difference* if what one is doing makes them feel good, blessed and fulfilled. It only matters that they stop doing it.

This way of acting, expressing one's own apprehension and affection, is *psychiatric* even if it doesn't use medications secretly dissolved in milk and doesn't end in a forced hospital admission. It is *psychiatric* for the logic that moves it and for the hypocrisy that justifies it.

There's a way of acting that, on the contrary, doesn't move its steps from *denying* someone else's experience. It's a way of acting that begins from doubting the true nature of reality, that doesn't practice certainties but takes risks in a dialogue with the other's certainties. A kind of interfering that is by *coming out into the open*. Accepting to accompany the other in their quest and be part of it. Asking oneself: *"Whatever will the Holy Grail seeker need?"* Perhaps just a safe place where to rest and regain strength in order to start again. And then cues, signs and encounters that point out the path to follow. They will need a car, someone who helps them climb over walls, cover distances, enter houses, break into private properties without being discovered and arrested. They will need money, suitable clothes, pen and paper, and so on... There's thousands of things to do *with* and *for* the other, if we accept to give credit to them, to be close to them, to understand without explanation.

The antipsychiatric way of acting doesn't aim at changing the other's way of thinking, acting and being. It aspires to build bridges of *inter/ference* between the world of *what's possible*, in which we commonly live, and the countless worlds of *what's impossible*, in which we can project our body and our mind. It's not interested in *reasoning with* the Grail seeker, in normalising his sleeping pattern, in making them resemble an office worker. It rather tries to experiment other forms of coexistence, communication and free exchange between people.

This radicality has got nothing to do with psychiatry, its history and its logic. The experience of the Italian *alternative* psychiatry, headed by Basaglia and the Law 180[4], has nothing to do with *antipsychiatry*. Basaglia's experience, in fact, moves its steps in the wake of *medical* research for a *cure* of *mental illness*. Even though its strategies, its techniques and its treatment facilities tend to resemble more and more the places of daily exchange, its logic at the basis of its interventions is always the one of *normalization* of the mind and the body of its *involuntary* patients.

It won't be necessary anymore to lock up the Grail

---

[4] **Basaglia Law (Law 180)** (Italian: *Legge Basaglia, Legge 180*) is the Italian Mental Health Act of 1978 which signified a large reform of the psychiatric system in Italy, contained directives for the closing down of all psychiatric hospitals and led to their gradual replacement with a whole range of community-based services, including settings for acute in-patient care. The Basaglia Law is the basis of Italian mental health legislation. The principal proponent of Law 180 and its architect was Italian psychiatrist Franco Basaglia. The Parliament of Italy enacted Law 180 on May 13, 1978, and thereby initiated the gradual dismantling of psychiatric hospitals. Implementation of the psychiatric reform law was accomplished in 1998 which marked the very end of the state psychiatric hospital system in Italy. The Law has had worldwide impact as other countries took up widely the Italian model. (Translators' note)

seeker. It will suffice that they will limit their search to the daytime, that they learn to talk about something else, that they let themselves being convinced to attend a day program for socialization where they can draw their secret maps to reach the Grail or write their own verses, tend the crop or produce small crafts to rehabilitate and feel *useful*... At night one will *help* them to sleep with medications in order to safeguard them from the risk of wandering in an *unproductive* way following their fantasies.

They will never be left alone. The seeker therefore will *seem* free to do and undo as they like, but they won't be free to *seek* anymore. That is equivalent to saying that they will be like a fish that is free to move as much as needed, but not to *swim*.

Everything will *seem* in order as long as the seeker will conform to the plan. If they will start to be awake at night, refuse medications, walk away from home without permission, refuse to cooperate with their workers, follow their instinct and that voice that is calling them to the *mission impossible*, then the alternative psychiatry will reserve a treatment to them that isn't any different from the (mis)treatments of the mental institutions. Isolation, humiliation, chemical lobotomy, enslavement. Involuntary admissions, even though time-limited and performed in *renewed* facilities, are experiences of personal annihilation that wipe out the possibility to resume having a say in our life.

Methods change, the purpose stays the same: the seeker *heals* when they give up seeking. The simple truth that a seeker gives up only when they have found, never entertains the mind of a psychiatrist (whether it is an alternative one or not). The psychiatrist doesn't see their search, but only a series of uncoordinated, irrational and senseless behaviours. The psychiatrist can't, is not capable of accepting the existence of the Holy Grail, or believing that the seeker has been *chosen*. The only thing they see is the danger and the risk the seeker runs by exposing himself to the night, to the city, to fantasy.

Of course not everybody seeks the Holy Grail. There are those who are invaded and tortured by diabolic entities, who feel they have transformed; those who see others change shape; those who live fearing the end of the world; those who feel that somebody wants to kill them... Experiences change sign, lives are diverse: the psychiatric indications stay the same. Do *not* listen, do *not* see, do *not* understand, do *not* believe, do *not* get out, do *not* shout, do *not* talk, do *not* think. The treatments put to use are, here as well, a mixture of *distraction* and *punishment*.

The psychiatric way of acting is moved by a grim and inhuman unwillingness to believe. Psychiatry not only doesn't give credit to its victims' experiences but, by reflex, it doesn't even share the distress those experiences sometimes produce. If diabolic entities do not exist, psychiatry argues, your terror is *unmotivated*.

If there's no *reason* for it, you *can't* be scared: your terror *doesn't* exist, it's only a fantasy that was created by the *illness* that you have to be *cured* of. Here as well a simple truth doesn't occur to the psychiatrist: those who are scared need to be *protected*, not *cured*.

Alternative psychiatrists often state that they use hospital admissions and medications in order to *protect* people. But it's worth to ask: *from whom* or *from what*? Normally from themselves, from the illness, from the life that they would like to live. Psychiatrists are not interested in demons. The *cures* serve the purpose of preventing us to react to things that do not exist. So, while we are stuck in a bed, tied to an IV drip, the demons, cruel and undeterred, are free to torment us.

The psychiatric callousness and inhumanity arises indeed from this dealing with human experiences as if they were foreign bodies, without any reference to the people who live those experiences.

As a consequence, one can lock up Angela, who is terrified by the nerve gas that pervades her home, one can abandon her in unknown places, stripped of her clothes and her belongings, one can feed with her the eyes and the bodies of strangers, forcing her to live without defence, with terror and fear, exposed to every danger.

Psychiatric interfering doesn't do anything, nothing

indeed, to prevent the gas to reach her. There's no nerve gas in her home: it's an *hallucination*, a *delusion*, an *inanity*. Angela *can't* suffer from something that is not there and can't hurt her. The psychiatric paradox states that the more Angela speaks out against the *tormentors* the more she is *punished*, the more she keeps asking for help, the more is considered *senseless*, the more she is afraid, the more she gets locked up.

Not just that. Angela, from nerve gas *victim*, will become *tormentor* of her family. She will drive her parents to despair, forcing them to sleepless nights in search of the spots from where the nerve gas is coming out. She will engage with them in endless discussions and huge fights in order to convince her to take her *medications*. She will go into hiding in her bedroom. She won't eat. She will seek refuge on the roof in order to escape those who want to kill her or drive her crazy.

Psychiatry dismisses all of this in two words: *persecutory delusion*. No one goes in search of the *persecutors*. No one defends Angela from them. There is no *persecutors*. Furthermore, psychiatry and persecution often coincide. Destroying her *credibility* serves also the purpose of allowing psychiatry to *cure* her without any limits or control.

Lobotomy, a brutal torture? Electroshock, a violent act? Mental institution, an extermination camp? For decades psychiatry has transformed these cruelties in *persecutory fantasies* of its victims. One cannot expect help from those who practice *persecution*, one cannot expect that they would recognize it.

SECOND INSTRUCTION: SEARCH FOR THE PERSECUTORS

Antipsychiatry finds itself often linked with accusations of denying people's suffering. It is said that those who don't accept the idea of the existence of *mental illness*, in fact, deny the suffering of the other and abstain from giving help to people who need it. I state, on the contrary, that in the antipsychiatric action there's the acknowledgement and full respect of someone else's experience. There's the act of taking direct responsibility for the challenge that the other's way of feeling, enjoying or suffering raises against our concept of reality and feelings.

Antipsychiatry doesn't avoid facing the nerve gas. It doesn't deny the *reality* and *truth* of Angela's terror. It aims at searching together with Angela for *credible* defences from the gas and locating its source to destroy it. It's the instinctive, natural and meaningful way of acting of those who find themselves in the situation of having to defend themselves from an *impossible* attack.

Psychiatry doesn't identify itself only with its practices, its workers or its institutions. It represents a way to *deny* which is widespread in our culture and is acted as the *norm*.

Antipsychiatry, on the contrary, comes from the practice of men and women who have tried to make sense of the huge amount of life experiences and knowledge that doesn't agree with the common way of seeing and being.

What are *delusions*, if not attempts to systematize the knowledge that comes to human beings from the activation of different perceptual channels, or integrating the five senses? And what are *symptoms*, if not attempts to respond, by trial and error, to paradoxes that such knowledge and experiences present to us?

We need to give a *meaning* to what happens to us. When the experience is such that it activates *extra-usual realities*, we can't expect to manage staying *sensible*. Did Francis' way of thinking seem *delirious* to the Assisi merchant? Striking and pathological his getting undressed? Unintelligible his relinquishment of reality? What would we have done had we been in the same situation? Would they have convinced us to reverse our decision? To take a break, to seek medical attention, psychotherapy?

The experience of the nerve gas or the *voice* of god, activates our body and our mind to a level in which words lose their meaning and power. They are experiences that make us new (blessed or terrified), free from the chains of *reason* and *common sense*. Home, work, money and future: how empty and incomprehensible sounds they must have seemed to Francis' ears! As empty and incomprehensible as the words that we do our utmost to whisper, shout, suggest to Angela.

Perhaps the matter is not to do our utmost to avoid people *going crazy*. How useless, senseless and cruel is such an idea. The matter is to try and make it *possible*, developing strategies and identifying *guides* who are able to accompany people in this journey.

Actually, psychiatrists don't have the experience, they know nothing of the things they maintain they know how (or want) to *cure*. Their *ignorance* becomes the *norm*; therefore everything they can't understand becomes *senseless*, everything they can't accept becomes *obscure*, everything they can't (ex)pound becomes pathological.

THIRD INSTRUCTION: ACTING INCOMPREHENSIBILITY AS INCOMPREHENSION

Those who are not in the *right* are not necessarily in the *wrong*. Most of the behaviours we can't understand become clear if we accept to take into account the views and experiences of the other. It is not a coincidence that the use of psychiatry decreases in proportion to the increase of our attention to the experiences of others. It's easy to propose psychiatric hospitalizations and psychotropic drugs for those who are *not themselves anymore*. It becomes emotionally impossible to put into the hands of psychiatry someone whose *reasons* we recognize and with whom we feel we still have a relationship of sense and affection.

There are countless acts of *daily* antipsychiatry, not theorized, but moved by the passions and relationships that bind us. They are acts of resistance ranging from keeping the pill under the tongue and then spit it out, to saving our loved ones from hospitalization *against* medical advice. An act that claims the right to be who you are, to communicate what you believe, to remain human beings.

It is easy to hospitalize Anna if she is heard every night screaming and threatening to kill herself. It is sensible to think that you are helping her by keeping her under control and calm with the *treatment*. You are saving her life.

Everything seems in order until we pay attention and listen to her words, until we ask: *"Why is she screaming?"* or *"Why does she want to die?"* Anna answers, she still wants to speak to the deaf and show her pain to the blind. There's a man, there's god, there's a voice that attacks her, insults her, threatens her, dishonours her. A disembodied being that nobody sees, no wall or gate can stop, no man can block. He is dominating her and she has no escape. Only the last resort: getting rid of her body to get rid of him.

Those who use psychiatry want to sleep at night. They don't want to be touched by the invisible presences that sometimes brush against us and they want to shut their mouth. They don't want to feel the gaze of death spying on us. There's nothing threatening her. She is threatening us. We are afraid; it is this *terror* that feeds the *voice* of psychiatry.

Among the countless techniques, strategies, tricks that Anna has developed in recent years to hold off, communicate with or to silence his persecutor, no one is taken seriously. On the contrary, her strategies are used by psychiatrists to make the diagnosis of schizophrenia she is labelled with.

Those who develop material or mental actions to address realities that psychiatry considers non-existent, is considered to be *mentally ill* and what they do, think, say is considered to be *pathological symptoms*. If Anna takes position against her *persecutor*, she is *delusional*. If she keeps aside and reduces contact with anything that hurts her, she is *autistic*. If she reacts by increasing the opportunities for socialization and relationship, she is *euphoric*. If she tries to feel positive entities that protect her from her persecutor, she is *hallucinated*.

Antipsychiatric action coincides perfectly with the acts that psychiatry calls *psychopathological*. It is the attempt to understand and have an effect on what happens to us and of us, without denying the facts or our experiences. What is commonly seen and treated as pure madness, it is actually research and testing of the truth, the meaning and the consequences of other ways of being in the world. Therefore, antipsychiatric is Francis of Assisi's adventure, Nino's dreaming, Antonio's urine that wets the neat floors of the new psychiatry, Carlo's wandering, Alberto's statues of faeces...

FOURTH INSTRUCTION: DO NOT CREATE RESERVATIONS

The history of psychiatry is the history of the attempts to avoid the encounter, the exchange and the contamination between the *real* and the *impossible*. History of the places - material and symbolic - where it isolates and controls the *infection* and the *mutiny* of human conscience.

If, throughout the mental asylums period, psychiatry justifies this exclusion with the need to protect the social order from madness, today, in the era of democratic psychiatry, this is done to protect people from reality. Places and excuses change, the process of systematic destruction of the social and emotional life of his victims remains intact. Too *dangerous* before, too *sensitive* now, never free to live their own lives or make their own choices.

The humanization of psychiatry has reconsidered this *mandate* of exclusion, going beyond the idea of concentration or imprisonment in total institutions of those infected, focusing on the development of a widespread social control network. The logic is to transform the body, the mind and the existence of every single *infected* in his prison, his straitjacket, his total institution. To neutralize every possibility to act, find allies, hear and be heard.

Psychiatric wards, clinics, residential homes, community care units... All the places institutionally responsible for *psychiatric* therapy, they only represent the visible outposts of the war of psychiatric invasion in our lives. There are no *places* anymore where you can take refuge in. Our homes can be turned into wards, our friends into nurses, our body into prison.

If Carmelo was tied to prevent him from acting and to force him to change his opinion, Arturo can be locked in a bed by incapacitating substances. Modern psychiatry is not satisfied that Arturo is punished or changes his mind, his critical skills and judgment. Only when he is made *incapable* of will, he will be *released* and entrusted to the care and control of personnel that is trained to not get involved nor touched by his humanity, reason, imagination. His body and his mind won't respond to his orders anymore, but to medical prescriptions.

The victims of post-asylum psychiatry are imprisoned in a

separated reality where playing, working and relationships are managed by others. A reality that reproduces the times and places of daily life as if they were real. Friendships, the trips, the laughter, the home, work, relationships, music, affections are duplicated... Everything *must* look real, but not be real. Psychiatric services users are second class people and a second class life must be built for them, a life that is devoid of the truth, strength and pain of real lived life.

It is difficult to convey what kind of subtle violence lurks behind this *alternative* way of doing psychiatry. It is difficult to make you feel the tragic *continuity* between the rusted grates of the asylums and the lace curtains of the residential rehabilitation services. It is difficult to show the direct filiation between lobotomy and psychotropic drugs. The identity of action between the rough mental hospital nurses and entertainers/occupational therapists of rehabilitation centres.

Everything seems so human. Everything seems so real. In rehabilitation centres there's the lounge, the TV, the kitchen, the rocking chair, the balconies with views of the city centre... In Social Enterprises, work *feels just like* work, it gives toil and sweat. The land that is cultivated *looks* real. The money that is earned *seems* real and it *looks like* they accept it at the café. The pills they give *look just like* real medicines. Even the doctors *seem* medics and the nurses *look just like* nurses. Everything *appears* real, even the smile of the entertainer who *seems really* happy to see us doodling for hours with colours that *appear* to be painting. Even the doctors *look like* they are listening to us, they understand us and they want to help us. Everything *seems* normal as long as you are convinced that it is. If you have a doubt and you express it, there's someone right there jumping up and telling you: *"Better than staying in a mental hospital"*. It's not an observation, it's a threat.

The *infected* live outside everyday life even when they get a coffee at the café next to us. The noise of their cup comes from another world. A world with no relationships and affection. A life which makes no sense and with no chance to share what is important to us or to do what we know or want. A life of compliance where anybody, no matter how lousy, seedy or cruel, can choose *for* us. A life on probation, subject to a constant brainwashing to make us forget *who* we are, and subject to a permanent re-education and normalization program. Threatened and ridiculed. At the mercy of our *protectors*.

The Grail seeker has no choice: he either gives up the Grail or he gives up his life. For those who don't *normalize* special programs are ready, involuntary admission, seclusion cell, guardianship... With or without the mental asylums, psychiatry always has the power and the resources to erase our lives with the stroke of a pen.

A psychiatry that is *alternative* to the mental asylum doesn't exist. Psychiatry is always *alternative* to human relations, to interpersonal exchange, to being human. Where psychiatry is, people are not *possible*. It's not possible that they speak freely, exchange views, influence each other, understand or misunderstand each other, love or hurt each other. It's not possible that they choose when to sleep and with whom, where to go and why, who or what they are.

Antipsychiatry is the act of reclaiming one's life. Which is what psychiatric *coerced* people have been practicing for years when they escape from their residential homes/prisons or from psychiatric services, when they jump off the moving municipal police car or run away from the training courses for deviants, from rehabilitation centres or from their monthly injections. Human beings that prefer the street, hunger, risk, pain, rather than pretending to live. Real hunger, real cold, real pain, real friendship, real violence. On the street you find more people willing to believe and accept you than you will find in any place that is designated to help. It only matters what you are, what you do. Outside of the psychiatric control, people become again visible, practical, real. What we see could unsettle us, confuse us, embarrass us: but it's what those people are. We could accept it or not, but we owe the Grail seeker the same respect that we demand for our job, our ideals, our feelings.

Antipsychiatric action does not create reservations. Places to protect people *from* reality. It doesn't build *commonplaces* to understand and contain the *impossible* human experiences. It's not a theory that explains, but a practice that comprehends by acting and acts by comprehending.

Antipsychiatric action is the invasion of daily reality in order to negotiate spaces of existence and movement for everybody. It doesn't duplicate the cafes, the homes, work, the parties, the relationships. It doesn't impose a way of life. It doesn't confuse the café assistant with the Grail seeker. It doesn't say that the seeker is in the *right* and the café assistant in the *wrong*. It tries to make their *choices* possible, without the existence of one meaning the *end* of the other.

FIFTH INSTRUCTION: ACTION

The instructions to use antipsychiatry are instructions to not be used by psychiatry. Instructions that suggest to see people for who they are and their actions for what they say. Stopping to use psychiatry means starting to use our eyes, our hands, our minds, our sensitivity to try and get in touch with people and experiences that we have ceased to feel, touch, think or understand.

Without our consent and our support, the Grail seeker can't be institutionalized, Anna can't be insulted, Anna can't be *cured*, Arturo can't be stopped, Carmelo can't be buried in a mental institution.

Antipsychiatry doesn't have specialists, organizations, techniques or cures. It doesn't make the Grail seeker reason or make Angela stop screaming. It wants to give them consideration and respect. It wants to act to help them seek the Grail or stop the nerve gas.

The *how to do it* is up to us, to our creativity, to our passion, to our humanity and intuition. I don't think it's easy, I say it is *possible*. After all we can't continue to accept that psychiatry solves for us the conflict between those who sleep at night and those who don't, between those who believe in the papal infallibility and those who believe that olive trees are the antennas of god on earth, between those who state that private property is a theft and those who say that someone stole their thoughts, between those who invest in the stock market and those who drive nails in all the holy icons of the city...

The incomprehensibility and the danger of *madness* are very small compared to the terror of psychiatric normalization. The psychiatric solution is always iniquitous, absurd and inhuman. If Sara drives her nails on the icon of our Lady of Help, psychiatry drives a lancet into her brain or a needle into her veins.

There are no *victims* and *executioners*. We are there too, on the roadside, while they take away the Grail seeker.

We are Angela's frightened neighbours, Carmelo's former high school classmates, Sara's speechless parishioners. We think we are only *unqualified* and random witnesses. On the contrary, we are the *instigators* of what happens, no less thoughtless, innocent and fearful than those nurses that execute the order to grab, hold, lock up and monitor their fellow human beings.

On our silence asylums were built. On our fear, psychiatric practices. You cannot step aside or get out of it. We are all recruited in this inhuman and fratricidal war. Terrified by the idea of an invisible, unpredictable and cruel enemy.

Deserting is not enough. One has to take a stand. Not execute the orders. Not wear uniforms or white coats. Not use our body anymore in order to prevent others from seeking. Not stop their body and mind. Not confuse the reasons. Continue to persist in wanting to remain human beings.

BIBLIOGRAPHY

1. ANTONUCCI G., *Il pregiudizio psichiatrico*, Eleuthera, Milano 1989 - *The Psychiatric Prejudice*

2. ANTONUCCI G., *Critica al giudizio psichiatrico*, Sensibili alle foglie, Roma 1993 - *Critique of psychiatric judgment*

3. ANTONUCCI G., *Contrappunti*, Sensibili alle foglie, Roma 1993 - *Counterpoints*

4. BREGGIN P. *Elettroshock*, Feltrinelli, Milano 1983 - *Electroshock: Its Brain-Disabling Effects, Springer, NY 1979*

5. BUCALO G., *Dietro ogni scemo c'è un villaggio*, Sicilia Punto L, Ragusa 1993 - *Behind every idiot there is a village*

6. BUCALO G., *Malati di niente*, Calusca Grafton, Milano 1996 - ~~In~~Sane *("Mentally ill" can be translated as "Malati di mente", and "niente" in Italian means "nil", "nothing" - Translators' Note)*

7. BUCALO G., DIzionARIO ANTIPSICHIATRICO , Sicilia Punto L, Ragusa 1997 - *ANTYPSYCHIATRIC DIctionARY*

8. BUCALO G., *Sentire le voci*, Sicilia Punto L, Ragusa 1998 - *Hearing Voices*

9. CESTARI R., *L'inganno psichiatrico*, Sensibili alle foglie, Roma 1994 - *The psychiatric scam*

10. CHAMBERLIN J., *Da noi stessi*, Primerano, Roma 1990 - *On Our Own, USA 1977*

11. COOPER D., *Grammatica del vivere*, Feltrinelli, Milano 1977 -*Grammar of Living, Penguin 1994*

12. COOPER D., *Psichiatria e antipsichiatria*, Armando, Roma 1978 - *Psychiatry and Antipsychiatry, Paladin 1967*

13. COOPER D., *Il linguaggio della follia*, Feltrinelli, Milano 1979 - *The Language of Madness, Penguin 1978*

14. COPPOLA A., ANTONUCCI G., *Il telefono viola contro i metodi della psichiatria*, Eleuthera, Milano 1995 – *The Purple Telephone Line Against the Methods of Psychiatry*

15. COTTI E., VIGEVANI R., *Contro la psichiatria*, La Nuova Italia, Firenze 1970 – *Against Psychiatry*

16. DE ROSSI R., *C'era una volta... storia del marinaio d'oltremare,* Coop. Apache, Roma 1986 – *Once Upon a Time... Story of the Overseas Sailor*

17. FORTI L., a cura di, *L'altra pazzia*, Feltrinelli, Milano 1975 – *The Other Madness*

18. FOUCALT M. *La casa della follia,* in Basaglia F., *Crimini di pace,* Einaudi, Torino 1975 – *The Mad House, in Basaglia F., Peace Crimes*

19. FOUCAULT M. *L'ordine del discorso*, Einaudi, Torino 1980 – *The Discourse on Language*

20. FRAME J., *Dentro il muro*, Interno giallo, Milano 1990 – *Inside the wall*

21. LAING R.D., ESTERSON A., *Normalità e follia nella famiglia*, Einaudi, Torino 1970 – *Sanity, Madness and the Family, Tavistock Publications, 1964*

22. LAING R.D., *Considerazioni sulla psichiatria*, in Basaglia F., *Crimini di pace*, Einaudi, Torino 1975 – *Reflections on Psychiatry, in Basaglia F., Peace Crimes*

23. LAING R.D. *Intervista sul folle e il saggio*, Laterza, Bari 1970 – *Interview on the mad and the wise*

24. LAING R.D. *Al di là della psichiatria*, Newton Compton, Roma 1970 – *Beyond psychiatry*

25. LAING R.D. *La politica dell'esperienza*, Feltrinelli, Milano 1980 – *The Politics of Experience, Penguin 1967*

26. MILLET K., *Il trip della follia*, Kaos, Milano 1994 – *The Loony-Bin Trip, 1990*

27. ONNIS L., LO RUSSO G., *La ragione degli altri*, Savelli, Roma 1979 – *The Reason of Others*

28. SHATZMAN M., *Storia di Ruth*, Feltrinelli, Milano 1990 – *The Story of Ruth, 1980*

29. SHATZMAN M., *La famiglia che uccide*, Milano 1973 – *Soul Murder: Persecution in the Family, Randomhouse, New York 1973*

30. SZASZ T., *Il mito della malattia mentale*, il Saggiatore, Milano 1966 – *The Myth of Mental Illness, 1961*

31. SZASZ T., *Disumanizzazione dell'uomo*, Feltrinelli, Milano 1981 - *Ideology and Insanity: Essays on the Psychiatric Dehumanization of Man*

32. SZASZ T., *La psichiatria a chi giova?*, in Basaglia F., *Crimini di pace*, Einaudi, Torino 1975 – *Psychiatry, Who Benefits from it?, in Basaglia F., Peace Crimes*

33. SZASZ T., *I manipolatori della pazzia*, Feltrinelli Milano 1981 – *The Manipulators of Madness, 1981*